Retirement Planning

Smart Moves for a Secure Future

Table of Contents

Chapter 1. Introduction

In this Special Report, "Retirement Planning: Smart Moves for a Secure Future," we bring you an exciting and crucial guide to securing your golden years. This easy-to-follow guide is brimming with actionable advice, practical strategies, and well-researched insights on how to systematically plan for your retirement. This is not just another dreary, technical manual, but a vibrant, heartening roadmap to financial independence in your post-career life. Planning for retirement might seem daunting now, but after diving into our upbeat and cheerfull guide, you'll emerge feeling motivated and driven, well-equipped to make informed decisions that secure your comfort and relief in the future. So get your hands on this report, for a worry-free, well-deserved retirement you can truly look forward to.

Chapter 2. Understanding the Basics of Retirement Planning

Let's START to understand the fundamentals of planning for retirement by delving deep into the core concepts involved. It's essential that you get a firm grasp on these before moving on to more advanced strategies.

2.1. Retirement: What Does It Really Mean?

Retirement isn't simply a period of unemployment that naturally follows the end of your career. It's a time for you to enjoy the fruits of your labor, to relax, to explore and engage in hobbies, and to focus on your personal growth and happiness, without the pressure of a 9-to-5 routine. For many, it's a new stage of life filled with potential and opportunities. You're not working less, you're simply working differently.

But to get there, you must prepare diligently and make thoughtful financial choices throughout your working years. That can ensure your post-career years are as content, stress-free, and fulfilling as they can be.

2.2. Saving Vs. Investing: Clearing the Confusion

Many people use the terms 'saving' and 'investing' interchangeably, but they are indeed two different things. Saving is the act of setting aside a portion of your income regularly, which is kept in a secure and easily accessible place, such as a savings account. Investing, on the other hand, involves putting your money into assets that are expected to yield returns over time, such as stocks, bonds, mutual funds, or real estate.

In the context of retirement planning, you must understand that savings alone may not be enough. The cost of living is increasing steadily, and what seems like a significant sum today may not hold the same value in the future. Therefore, a strategic mix of savings and investments can help you build a robust retirement fund.

2.3. The Role of Social Security

Social Security is a government-run program that provides benefits to retirees, disabled individuals, and families of retired or disabled workers. While this is a crucial source of income post-retirement for many, it's vital not to overly depend on it. Several factors, such as the financial health of the program, changes in government policies, and your eligibility, will affect the amount of benefit you receive.

Relying solely on Social Security benefits can lead to financial hardship during retirement. These benefits should be a safety net, supplementing your personal savings and investments.

2.4. Understanding Life Expectancy

You likely don't relish thinking about your mortality, but doing so is crucial when planning for retirement. Keep in mind, advances in medicine and healthcare, among other factors, are increasing life spans. Therefore, it's essential to plan for a retirement that could last 20 years or more.

Not planning for a longer life span can result in exhaustion of retirement savings, leaving an individual with limited financial resources in their advanced years.

2.5. Your Retirement Plan: Defined Benefit vs. Defined Contribution

A retirement plan provided by your employer is a vital part of your retirement strategy. The two most common types are Defined Benefit (DB) and Defined Contribution (DC) plans.

DB plans, often called pension plans, offer a predefined amount of money at retirement based on your salary and years of service.

DC plans, like 401(k) or 403(b), allow you to make regular contributions, often with a matching amount from your employer. The money invested grows over time. At retirement, the accumulated funds are withdrawn as you wish.

Whether you have a DB, DC, or both, understanding how they work can help you plan better.

2.6. The Magic of Compounding

Compounding is an essential concept in retirement planning. By reinvesting the returns you earn on your investments, the original amount multiplies at an increasing rate over time. This growth is exponential rather than linear, meaning your wealth grows faster as time goes on.

For example, if you start saving $200 a month at a 6% interest rate from age 25, you could accumulate a sum of around $400,000 by age 65. Leave it until age 40 to start, and you'd only have around $130,000 by 65.

This example illustrates why it's vital to start planning and investing for retirement as early as possible. Waiting can drastically reduce your potential returns, making it more challenging to achieve your retirement goals.

2.7. The Importance of Diversification

Diversification is the strategy of investing your money across a variety of asset classes (such as stocks, bonds, and real estate) to spread the risk. The rationale is that different types of investments perform differently at various times and having a diverse portfolio can lessen the impact of a poor performing investment on your total returns.

By diversifying your retirement funds, you can better manage risk and increase the chances of achieving long-term growth.

As we conclude this segment, remember that knowledge is only the first step. Applying these principles consistently throughout your working life is what will make the difference when it comes to ensuring a secure and fulfilling retirement. The earlier you start, the better the prospects for your golden years. Now, you're well-equipped to navigate your way through the maze of retirement planning.

Chapter 3. Assessing Your Financial Status: Key to Efficient Planning

One of the vital initial steps in crafting your retirement plan is accurately assessing your current financial status. Having a clear understanding of where you stand financially will help pinpoint what steps need to be taken to reach your retirement goals. Some key aspects you need to focus on include understanding your assets, liabilities, expenses, income sources, cash flow, and net worth.

3.1. Understanding Your Assets

To begin, it's crucial to understand your assets. Assets are everything you own that has a monetary value. They can be tangible like a house, car, or other valuable possessions, or intangible, such as your investments (stocks, bonds, mutual funds), retirement accounts (IRA, 401(k), annuities), and cash savings.

A detailed list of your assets is essential. Start by making an inventory of all your tangible and intangible assets, noting their estimated current market value. This exercise will not just provide you with a clear picture of your overall wealth but also enable you to strategize how best to utilize these assets to generate income during your retirement.

3.2. Evaluating Your Liabilities

In addition to assets, understanding the full extent of your liabilities is key. Liabilities include your mortgage balance, personal loans, credit card obligations, car loans, or any other debt. Calculate your total outstanding liabilities to have a clear idea of the obligations that may impact your financial health.

This inventory of your liabilities will help you devise strategies to pay them off, aiming for a debt-free retirement. It's not unusual to carry some debt into retirement, but too much liability can destabilize your financial security.

3.3. Expenses Tracking

OBSERVING YOUR CURRENT AND POTENTIAL FUTURE EXPENSES is another critical element of taking stock of your financial setup. It helps estimate your cost of living during retirement.

Analyze your current spending habits. This analysis can be broken down into two categories: fixed expenses (rent, mortgage, utility bills) and variable expenses (drinks, dining out, holidays). Think about the lifestyle you aim to maintain post-retirement, and assess predictable future expenses such as healthcare, which typically increase with age.

3.4. Identifying Income Sources

Another crucial factor is identifying your various income sources. Besides a pension or Social Security, other potential income streams could include rental income, dividends from investments, withdrawal from retirement accounts, part-time work, or even a small business.

Compile all these sources and add them up. The total should ideally be sufficient to cover your retirement expenses at any given time. If there's a shortfall, strategizing how to boost income or decrease expenses becomes a critical part of the plan.

3.5. Cash Flow Analysis

A key tool in understanding your financial health is cash flow analysis. It involves scrutinizing your regular cash inflow (income) versus outflow (expenses). Having positive cash flow means generating more income than you're spending, which empowers savings and investment for retirement.

Check your cash flow regularly, ideally every month. It will provide you with an up-to-date picture of your financial health and guide your decision-making regarding whether there is room to save more or if you need to cut down expenses.

3.6. Calculating Net Worth

Your net worth is the value of your assets minus your liabilities. It serves as a financial snapshot, giving you a clear number that states your financial value. Regularly updating net worth calculations can track financial growth over time, reflect the effectiveness of your financial decisions, and substantiate your path to financial freedom post-retirement.

To conclude, assessing your financial situation can be complex, but it's a critical first step. Take your time to understand the numbers and what they mean for your future. If necessary, consult with a financial advisor to ensure you're interpreting your financial status correctly and crafting a pension scheme tailored to your needs. Your retirement deserves nothing less than your best preparation. Your well-informed choices today lay the blueprint for a secure future. This comprehensive analysis of your finances is your first victory in your journey to a worry-free retirement.

Chapter 4. The Power of Compounding: Start Early, Save More

One of the most potent tools at your disposal in the quest for a secure future, is something Albert Einstein famously referred to as the eighth wonder of the world: compound interest. Compounding is crucial to growing your wealth over the long term, and the earlier you begin, the more profound its effects.

4.1. Understanding Compounding

So what exactly is compounding? At its core, compounding refers to the cycle where you earn interest on your initial investment (principal), plus any interest that has previously accrued. You're effectively earning interest on your interest. In the world of finance, this is where the magic happens. Suppose you invest $1,000 at a 5% annual interest rate. In the first year, you'll earn $50 in interest. The following year, however, you'll earn interest not just on your original $1,000, but also on the added $50 from the previous year, bumping your interest earned to $52.50. That $2.50 may seem insignificant, but over time, this small increase results in exponential growth of your investment.

4.2. The Time Value of Money

Compounding is directly connected to the concept of the time value of money, which asserts that a dollar today is worth more than a dollar tomorrow. That's because the dollar you hold today can be invested to turn into more dollars in the future. This idea helps underscore the value of starting to save as early as possible.

4.3. The Rule of 72

An easy way to visualize the power of compounding is through the rule of 72, a simple mathematical formula used to estimate the doubling time of an investment. By dividing 72 by the rate of annual return, investors can get a rough estimate of how many years it will take for the initial investment to duplicate itself. For example, if your rate of return was 6%, your investment would double approximately every 12 years (72 ÷ 6).

4.4. Start Early

But when to start? The power of compounding is truly harnessed by starting to invest as early as possible. An extra ten years of saving and investing could represent hundreds of thousands, if not millions, of additional retirement dollars, simply by giving your money more years to grow and capitalize on the benefits of compounding.

We'll illustrate this with a quick example. Let's consider two investors, Alice, who starts investing at age 25, and Bob, who starts at 35. They both invest $5,000 per year at a 7% annual return rate until age 65. At retirement, Alice will have around $1.44 million, while Bob will have approximately $734,000. Although Bob invested the same amount per year as Alice, starting ten years later means he ended up with nearly half the amount Alice did at retirement.

4.5. Investing Regularly

More than just about starting early, the principle of compounding requires consistency. By consistently contributing to your savings or investment accounts, there is an inherently larger principal amount for the compound interest to work its magic on. This method of constant, periodic contributions is often referred to as dollar-cost averaging. It reduces the impact of volatility on the overall cost of investments, providing potential for increased long-term returns.

4.6. Reinvest Your Returns

Another key to maximizing the power of compounding is to reinvest your returns. If you're investing in assets that generate dividend and interest income, reinvesting that income back into additional assets can significantly enhance the rate at which your investment grows.

4.7. The Role of Tax-Advantaged Accounts

Using tax-advantaged accounts such as 401(k) plans, IRAs, or health savings accounts can also amplify the impact of compounding. These types of accounts typically offer tax-deferred or tax-free growth, which effectively allows your wealth to compound even faster.

Let's review an example. Assume that you make a $5,500 contribution to an IRA that generates a 7% annual return. After 30 years, without any additional contributions, that $5,500 would become approximately $41,900 in a tax-deferred account. In a taxable account, assuming a 15% tax rate on the yearly returns, that same $5,500 would only grow to about $28,600 over the same period.

Just as with our earlier examples, that's a significant difference when considered over a long time frame.

In conclusion, the power of compounding is an integral part of wealth building. However, its effectiveness decays with time, emphasizing the importance of starting early. The practice of consistently investing, reinvesting returns, and utilizing tax-advantaged accounts further enhances the blossoming effect of compounding, potentially securing a hearty retirement nest egg for the diligent investor. So, don't delay; start your journey today, and let the magic of compounding pave the path to your financial independence.

Chapter 5. Diversifying Your Investments: Not All Eggs in One Basket

Investing is not just about making more money or beating the market. It's about managing risk, aiming for a sustainable and acceptable level of returns and aligning your financial goals with your portfolio. Diversification is one of the key strategies used to manage risk.

5.1. The Concept of Diversification

To understand diversification, imagine a seesaw. Put all your investments on one side, and the risk is dramatically tilted. Spread out your investments on both sides, and it balances out. Diversifying your investment is like spreading your assets across several investments to balance the risk.

The goal of diversification is not necessarily to boost performance—it won't ensure gains or guarantee against losses. But once you choose to target a level of risk based on your goals, time horizon, and tolerance for volatility, diversification may provide the potential to improve returns for that level of risk.

5.2. The Importance of Diversification

A well-diversified portfolio can help to protect against the risks of individual asset classes. For example, a downturn in one type of asset, like stocks, can be offset by strength in another asset category, such as bonds.

Investment categories, including stocks, bonds, and cash, do not move up and down at the same time or at the same rate. Market conditions that cause one asset category to do well often cause another asset category to have average or poor returns. By investing in more than one asset category, you reduce the risk of losing money and your portfolio's overall risk of investment losses decreases.

5.3. How to Diversify Your Investments

Creating a diversified investment portfolio starts with allocating assets among different categories of investments. The three main asset classes are stocks, bonds, and cash. However, further diversification can be achieved by investing in subcategories within each major asset class. This might include different types of stocks, like large-cap, mid-cap, small-cap, international, or sector-specific stocks.

Table 1. Allocation Example

Type of Stock	Type of Bonds	Type of Cash
Large-cap	Government bonds	Saving Account
Mid-cap	Corporate bonds	Money market funds
Small-cap	Municipal bonds	Certificates of deposit (CDs)
International	Junk bonds	
Sector-specific	Bond funds	

Remember, it's important to diversify within each asset category as well. This is because different categories tend to perform differently under different market conditions.

5.4. Rebalancing: The Key to Maintain Diversification

Over time, some of your investments will grow faster than others, and some may even fall in value. This results in your asset allocation changing, which can cause your portfolio to stray from its target diversification. To prevent this, you should rebalance your portfolio periodically by selling investments in over-weighted categories and using that money to buy investments in under-weighted categories.

5.5. Investing in Mutual Funds and ETFs for Diversification

Investing in mutual funds or exchange-traded funds (ETFs) is an easy way to diversify your portfolio. These funds hold a wide range of stocks, bonds, or other investments. By purchasing shares in a mutual fund or ETF, you get access to a broad spectrum of assets, achieving diversification with a single transaction.

5.6. The Role of Alternative Investments

Besides stocks, bonds, and cash, you may want to consider alternative investments like real estate, commodities, or hedge funds. These can provide a further layer of diversification, as they tend to behave differently from traditional markets. However, keep in mind that these asset types can carry additional risks and are often not suitable for all investors.

5.7. The Risk of Over-Diversification

While diversification is key in investing, it is also possible to overdo it. Over-diversification occurs when you own so many assets that they overlap, increasing your costs and reducing your potential returns. However, striking a balance is vital and an expert financial advisor can help you ensure you have the right mix.

By understanding and implementing diversification, you're better equipped to navigate the uncertainties of the financial markets. Remember, diversification isn't just a one-time task—it's an ongoing process that should align with your evolving financial goals and risk tolerance.

This comprehensive diversification strategy will certainly play an instrumental role in shaping your secure financial future, offering you the retirement comfort you truly deserve.

Chapter 6. Pension Plans and Social Security: What You Need to Know

Understanding the essentials of pension plans and Social Security can mean the difference between struggling to make ends meet in retirement and sailing smoothly into a worry-free post-career life. With careful planning, you can maximize your retirement benefits and live those golden years in the comfort and ease you deserve.

6.1. Understanding Pension Plans

Pension plans, or defined benefit plans, provide retirees with a fixed, pre-established benefit for life. The payout you receive upon retirement depends on several factors, including your salary, years of service, and the terms of the plan itself.

In the private sector, two types of pension plans prevail: single-employer and multiemployer plans. Single-employer plans are established by one company for its employees, whereas multiemployer plans involve several employers working within the same or related industries.

Further, there are traditional and cash balance plans. A traditional pension plan calculates the employee's benefits using a formula that considers years of service and final salary. A cash balance plan, on the other hand, adds a set percentage of the employee's salary each year, plus interest charges.

6.1.1. Pros and Cons of Pension Plans

Given their defined benefit nature, pension plans offer the significant advantage of providing a reliable, fixed income during retirement.

This is a huge relief to retirees, as they can plan their expenses without worrying about fluctuating income.

On the flip side, the key disadvantage lies in the lack of control. The benefit amount is determined by a preset formula and does not account for personal investment risk tolerance or goals.

6.2. Understanding Social Security

Social Security is a federal program that provides benefits to retired workers, their survivors, and dependents. It is funded through payroll taxes imposed on both employees and employers under the FICA (Federal Insurance Contributions Act).

6.2.1. How is Social Security Benefit Calculated?

The Social Security Administration uses a formula that takes into account your 35 highest years of earnings. If you haven't worked for 35 years, zeroes are added to replace missing years, which can lower your ultimate benefit.

Your benefit at full retirement age is known as your Primary Insurance Amount (PIA). You can decide to start receiving benefits as early as 62 or as late as 70. If you start before your full retirement age, your benefits will be reduced; if you wait until after, your benefits will increase due to delayed retirement credits.

6.2.2. Pros and Cons of Social Security

Thanks to Social Security, you enjoy a somewhat predictable income stream in retirement. Plus, Social Security benefits are adjusted for cost of living, so inflation won't significantly erode your benefit's purchasing power.

The main drawback of Social Security is the uncertainty surrounding its future. Given the current rate of people drawing from Social

Security versus those paying into it, some worry about the longevity of the program.

6.3. Choosing Between Pension Plans and Social Security

Many employers offer pensions as a part of their overall compensation package. If you're lucky enough to have a choice between pension benefits and Social Security, you may be wondering which is better.

In general, pensions are considered more reliable since they provide a steady, known amount each month. Social Security, on the other hand, is susceptible to changes in government policy and economic instability.

But since each person's circumstances differ greatly, it's beneficial to run your unique figures through both systems to see what works better for you.

6.4. Act Now. Secure Your Retirement

Pension plans and Social Security are tools that can assure you a safe and comfortable retirement. But like all tools, their efficacy depends on understanding how they work and using them wisely. By making informed decisions, you can make your retirement dreams a reality.

Chapter 7. The Role of Insurance in Retirement Planning

Retirement planning is a multi-faceted effort involving a variety of components to ensure financial security, and among them, insurance plays a key role. Insurance provides a safety net for unexpected occurrences that could potentially pose a major financial risk.

7.1. Understanding the Importance of Insurance

Insurance isn't necessarily about investing but more about protecting yourself financially from risk. Insurance helps manage potential risk of significant financial loss caused by unpredictable circumstances such as disability, long-term illness, or death.

For the retired, or those close to retirement, it is crucial to mitigate these risks. The loss of income due to such setbacks could potentially hurl an individual into financial turmoil, especially when there are insufficient savings or assets to rely on. Insurance products can provide peace of mind that a safety net exists, ensuring risks are well taken care of.

7.2. Essential Insurance Types for Retirement Planning

There are several types of insurance that are particularly important during retirement. Each provides coverage for different life events, and together they form a crucial part of your retirement plan.

7.2.1. Life Insurance

Often people think they no longer need life insurance once they've retired. However, some retirees may still have dependents, or they wish to provide a financial legacy. This can necessitate maintaining a life insurance policy. Life insurance can offer a lump sum (death benefit) to your dependents when you pass away. This action can help to alleviate financial burdens like daily living expenses, any outstanding debts, or even estate taxes that your dependents might face without your financial support.

7.2.2. Health Insurance

In later years, medical expenses are perhaps the most unpredictable and potentially the most expensive outlays. To make things worse, aging often comes hand in hand with an increase in health-related issues. Medicare is an essential resource, but it doesn't cover everything. Out-of-pocket health-care costs, prescription drugs, dental and eye care are often not fully covered. Having health insurance or a supplemental policy can help to decrease these potential financial burdens. Furthermore, long-term care insurance is growing in significance as the average lifespan increases.

7.2.3. Long-Term Care Insurance

Long-term care insurance covers a range of services and supports for personal care needs. The U.S. Department of Health and Human Services reports that seven in ten people turning 65 today will need some form of long-term care in their remaining years. Long-term care can be incredibly costly, and neither health insurance nor Medicare provides comprehensive coverage for such care.

7.3. Analyzing the Cost-Benefit of Insurance in Retirement

A significant challenge in procuring insurance is determining the most cost-effective way to do so. The cost of insurance is based on risk analysis by the insurance entity. They estimate the likelihood of the insured event occurring, the potential payout, and the timeframe. These costs need to be evaluated against personal circumstances and the potential financial loss without insurance.

Insurance should be viewed as protection against a potential significant financial loss, rather than a gain. Life and disability insurance should be considered if dependents are involved. Health insurance, including long-term care coverage, should be highly considered due to potentially high health-related costs in later years.

It's important to shop around when considering insurance. Costs can vary considerably among insurance companies, so examining and comparing the details of different policies is crucial.

7.4. Conclusion

Retirement planning is not just about building a nest egg or capital investment; it is also about securing your finances against unforeseen setbacks that could potentially wipe out your savings. Insurance is an essential component of this defense strategy. It brings peace of mind by providing a safety net against events that could lead to significant financial loss. From life insurance to health or long-term care coverage, every policy has its unique role to play in a holistic retirement plan. So, as you plan for your golden years, do not underestimate the role of insurance. It isn't an unnecessary overhead but rather a lifeline when you need one most.

Remember, the ultimate goal is a retirement period that's fulfilling, financially secure, and as worry-free as possible. Insurance, when thoughtfully integrated into your retirement plan, helps pave the way for just that. The risks are real, and the relative cost of insurance coverage is low compared to the peace of mind and financial protection it affords.

23

Chapter 8. Effective Tax Planning Strategies for Retirement

Saving sufficient funds for your retirement is a primary financial goal everyone should focus on. Now, once you've stocked your financial pipeline with retirement savings, the challenge shifts to how to manage your taxes efficiently, because taxes can significantly impact your retirement income if proper planning strategies are not put in place.

8.1. Understanding the Tax Basics

Just as you've considered how to save and invest, understanding how taxes will affect your retirement funds comes down to being aware of the basics.

Firstly, your personal tax rate: recognize what tax bracket you currently fall into and how your withdrawals will be taxed when you retire. Depending on the types of retirement accounts you have, as well as the income you draw during retirement, you may find yourself in a lower or higher tax bracket.

Next, the nature of your retirement funds: different retirement accounts are taxed differently, and the most common types are taxable, tax-deferred, and tax free.

- Taxable accounts are standard brokerage accounts in which funds you contribute are already taxed. Investments grow tax-deferred until you sell them and the gains are then subject to capital gains tax rates.

- Tax-deferred accounts include most traditional retirement accounts like 401(k)s and traditional IRAs. Contributions made are often tax deductible, but any withdrawals made in retirement are taxed as regular income.

- Tax-free accounts include Roth 401(k)s and Roth IRAs, in which contributions are made after taxes, but the earnings and withdrawals are tax-free.

The main goal in tax planning for retirement should be to minimize the total taxes paid by managing taxable income and timing it optimally.

8.2. Diversify Your Tax Buckets

Diversifying your retirement accounts is a wise strategy, just as portfolio diversification reduces investment risk. Being tax-agnostic during the investment phase leaves you exposed to unpredictable future tax scenarios. Contribute to taxable, tax-deferred, and tax-free accounts to pull income from each in retirement. This strategy offers tax diversification and provides the ability to manipulate taxable income in retirement.

8.3. The Roth Conversion Strategy

Roth IRAs and Roth 401(k)s are potentially attractive options because future withdrawals will be tax-free. If you expect higher tax rates in retirement, a Roth conversion strategy could be a smart move.

A Roth conversion strategy involves moving funds from a traditional IRA into a Roth IRA. The converted amount will be subject to income tax in the year of the conversion. But going forward, your earnings can compound tax-free, and withdrawals made post retirement are also tax-free.

8.4. Utilizing the Standard Deduction

Through utilizing the standard deduction, you can reduce the amount of your income subject to taxation. The Tax Cuts and Jobs Act (TCJA) significantly increased the standard deduction. For 2022, the standard deduction is $12,950 for single filers, $25,900 for married couples filing jointly.

8.5. Timing Your Withdrawals

The timing of your withdrawals can play a significant role in minimizing your tax implications. Typically, withdrawing tax-deferred assets later in retirement and letting them compound over time can be advantageous.

Once you turn 72, the Required Minimum Distribution (RMD) rules dictate that you must start taking withdrawals from most types of tax-advantaged retirement accounts, which are then taxed.

Therefore, by carefully planning your strategic withdrawals during your early retirement years, you can limit the impact such distributions may have on your tax liability.

8.6. Use Tax-Efficient Fund Placement

The concept of tax-efficient fund placement is actually quite straightforward. It involves placing investments that are expected to be taxed at higher rates into accounts that provide a tax advantage, and placing investments taxed at lower rates into taxable accounts.

For example, bonds that generate regular interest payments could go into tax deferred or tax-free accounts while stocks (lower taxed investments) would perform better in a taxable account.

8.7. Gifting and Inheritance

It's also vital to understand the potential tax implications of bequests you plan to leave or gifts you intend to give, as it can dictate the best way to pass assets onto heirs.

In conclusion, tax planning for retirement doesn't have to be a daunting task. With the right strategies such as understanding tax basics, diversifying your tax buckets, considering a Roth conversion, utilizing the standard deduction, timing withdrawals carefully, using tax efficient fund placements and planning out gifting and inheritance, you can substantially decrease your tax liabilities and conserve more of your hard-earned retirement funds. Always consult with a tax professional or certified financial advisor before making any decisions about your retirement savings.

Chapter 9. Estate Planning: Ensuring Your Assets Go Where They Should

Passing on a legacy to your loved ones is the crowning achievement of financial success. But it's not as simple as just willing your possessions. With proper estate planning, you can ensure your assets are distributed as per your wishes and help your heirs bypass the cumbersome and costly probate process.

9.1. Decoding Estate Planning

Estate planning involves making plans in advance for the distribution of your assets after you pass away. The comprehensive process involves will creation, trusts, power of attorney, health care surrogate, taxation considerations, and life insurance, among other things. The cycle begins with understanding your assets' current standing and your final wishes for their distribution.

Begin by creating a detailed inventory of your current assets. These can include tangible assets such as real estate properties, cars, valuables, as well as intangible assets such as investments, insurance policies, and bank accounts. It's essential to update this inventory annually or after major life events like marriage, a new child, divorce, or death.

9.2. Crafting a Will

A will serves as the cornerstone of your estate planning. It outlines precisely how you wish to distribute your assets to your beneficiaries post your death. Without it, the state takes over the distribution, often causing unintended outcomes.

To create a will, enlist the services of an estate planning attorney. This professional can help you draft a legal will that stands the test of time, considering your particular needs. When writing a will, it's essential to nominate an executor, an individual who'll oversee the distribution of your assets as per your will. When choosing an executor, consider their organizational skills, integrity, and willingness to accept the responsibility.

9.3. Understanding Trusts

Trusts are another crucial tool for ensuring your assets reach your beneficiaries exactly the way you want. A trust allows a third party, a trustee, to hold and distribute assets to your beneficiaries as per your directives. There are various types of trusts available today, each serving different purposes.

- Living trusts allow you to remain in control of your assets during your lifetime, and your heirs can bypass probate upon your demise.

- Testamentary trusts only come into effect after your death, typically being part of your will.

- Irrevocable trusts protect your assets in the event of lawsuits or creditors' claims.

Consider speaking to a financial advisor or an estate planning attorney to identify which type of trust would best serve your needs.

9.4. Beneficiary Designations

Ensure you have named beneficiaries wherever possible, like in investment accounts, retirement plans, and insurance policies. Designated beneficiaries are a direct way of transferring assets and bypass probate. Keep your beneficiary designations updated, reflecting changes in your life like marriage, divorce, birth of a child, and death.

9.5. Estate Taxes and How to Minimize Them

Estate taxes can significantly erode your heirs' inheritance. However, strategic planning can lower, or even eliminate these taxes altogether. Understanding the tax laws around gift giving, for instance, can help you reduce the overall value of your taxable estate. As of now, you can make an annual gift of upto $15,000 per recipient without extending into taxable territory.

9.6. Establishing Power of Attorney and Health Care Surrogate

Estate planning isn't just about death; it's also about incapacitation. A power of attorney grants a trusted individual the legal authority to make financial decisions on your behalf if you're unable to do.

Likewise, a health care surrogate can make crucial health care decisions for you if you're incapacitated. It's crucial to discuss your desires with your surrogate, ensuring they carry out your wishes in such a situation.

9.7. Review and Update Your Plan Regularly

Your estate plan is a living document. Just like your life changes, so must your estate plan. An outdated estate plan might not serve its purpose. Regularly review and update your plan to reflect any changes in your assets, relationships, or wishes.

Estate planning can seem daunting, but it does not have to be. With a clear understanding of the process and the help of professionals, you can rest assured knowing your legacy is destined to go exactly where you intended.

Chapter 10. Adjusting Your Plan: Navigating Market Volatility and Emergencies

Market volatility and unexpected emergencies - these are unavoidable elements of life that can thwart even the best-laid financial plans. Whether it's a sudden dip in the stock market, a costly medical emergency, or the need for a substantial home repair, these unpredictable events can swiftly erode your retirement savings if your plan is not adjusted accordingly to navigate them.

10.1. Understanding Market Volatility

Market volatility, or the rate at which the price of an asset increases or decreases, is a common occurrence in any investment market. There's no escaping it if you are investing in stocks, bonds, mutual funds, or any other investment vehicles. While it may seem intimidating, understanding market volatility can actually empower you to make informed decisions regarding your retirement planning.

Historically, the markets increase in value over time. However, the journey is often characterized by periods of both rapid growth and significant downturns. Sharp downturns in the market can be particularly unsettling for retirees and those nearing retirement, as it can significantly reduce the value of their investments.

Nonetheless, it's important to remember that market volatility is a normal part of investing. Rather than panicking and pulling your investments out of the market during these periods of volatility, it can be more beneficial to ride out the storms. This is because the market typically recovers over time, and by remaining invested, you allow your assets the opportunity to recover and potentially grow.

However, with retirement being a major life event that requires substantial financial preparation, it may be wise to shift towards a conservative investment strategy as you near this phase. Depending on your risk tolerance, shifting your investments from high-risk options like stocks to lower-risk options such as bonds or index funds can help insulate your retirement fund from dramatic shifts due to market volatility.

Remember to consult with a financial advisor before making any major decisions about your investment strategy.

10.2. Building an Emergency Fund

Another common disruption to retirement planning comes in the form of unexpected emergencies. These can range from major health issues, sudden job loss, to costly home repairs, and they often come without warning.

To ensure that these unexpected costs do not drain your retirement savings, it's advisable to set up an emergency fund. An emergency fund is a stash of money set aside to cover the financial surprises life throws your way. It's essentially a safety net and can provide peace of mind knowing that you are financially protected against unforeseen mishaps.

Financial experts generally recommend saving enough in your emergency fund to cover three to six months' worth of living expenses. This money should be easily accessible, such as in a savings or checking account, rather than invested in assets that may be hard to liquidate quickly.

Once your emergency fund is set up, ensure to replenish it if you dip into it, thereby maintaining its intended purpose.

10.3. Adjusting Your Retirement Plan

Considering the looming possibility of market volatility and emergencies, it is vital to adjust your retirement plan regularly. This not only helps in keeping your plan aligned with your financial goals but also aids in navigating through uncertain times.

Your retirement plan is not a static document, but rather a dynamic compass, needing frequent adjustments to keep you on track. Regular reassessment allows you to identify any gaps, anticipate future challenges, and encapsulates the changed circumstances into it.

Regular adjustments may hinge upon factors like: - Changes in income or living expenses - Major life events like marriage, childbirth, or loss of a spouse - Changes in the market - Changes in tax laws - Unexpected emergencies or health issues

When adjustments are necessitated, a critical perspective without panic should be employed. If the markets are volatile, remember that it is a part of the economic cycle. If an emergency arises, use the emergency fund rather than dipping into your retirement savings. It may be tempting to react immediately and drastically, especially during market downturns. But choose your actions wisely and assess their long-term impacts on your retirement goals.

10.4. Working with a Financial Advisor

Because of the variability and complexity involved in managing market volatility and emergencies, it can be beneficial to work with a financial advisor. They can provide guidance and expertise, helping you make decisions that align with both your current financial situation and your retirement goals.

They can also play a critical role in helping you evaluate your risk tolerance and investment strategy, and adjust your retirement plan when necessary. Seek a financial advisor who understands your life goals and financial aspirations, and is proactive in adjusting your plan as required. Remember, the objective is not just about surviving during challenging times, but thriving through them to achieve a secured retirement.

In conclusion, navigating market volatility and emergencies requires flexibility in your retirement planning with a robust emergency fund as a safety net. Regular adjustments to your retirement plan can also help you remain on track. Understanding these nuances and engaging a financial advisor is crucial for your retirement planning to ensure a secure and financially independent future. Remember, these hurdles do not have to derail your plans for a peaceful and rewarding retirement. With proper preparation and active management, they can be minor detours on your road to a secure and enjoyable retirement.

Chapter 11. Living the Retirement Dream: A Guide to Managing Your Retirement Income

Managing your retirement income can be as rewarding as it is challenging. On one hand, you've likely accrued savings over decades in the workforce, which can provide financial stability. On the other, variables such as inflation and life expectancy can create a great amount of uncertainty.

11.1. Key Retirement Income Sources

To begin with, know that typical retirement income comes from the following sources:

1. Social Security

2. Retirement accounts (IRA, 401k)

3. Pensions

4. Part-time Work

5. Annuities

6. Real Estate Investments

Understanding where your retirement income is sourced from will aid in crafting a comprehensive and intuitive financial plan.

11.2. Optimizing Social Security Benefits

With Social Security being an important part of retirement income, it's essential you understand how to maximize its benefits. The age you start taking social security benefits directly impacts the monthly payments you receive. In general, the later you begin receiving benefits—up to age 70—the higher your monthly payments will be.

To determine the best age to start receiving Social Security, factor in your current health, life expectancy, need for immediate income, and any future financial obligations.

11.3. Evaluating Pension and Retirement Accounts

Besides Social Security, some individuals may have access to a pension, or defined benefit plan. If you have a pension, you'll need to decide whether to take a lump sum or recurring payments. This pivotal decision will impact your retirement in terms of taxation and possible lifespan of the pension.

Combine and evaluate this pension with other retirement savings accounts like the 401k or IRA. The importance lies in understanding the distribution of these funds. Traditional IRA and 401k disbursements count as taxable income, whereas Roth IRAs do not. Understanding taxation will greatly influence the income you'll receive post-tax in retirement.

Consider working with a Certified Financial Planner, or doing a deep dive into tax policies to make informed decisions.

11.4. Planning for Longevity Risk

Life expectancy is a significant variable in retirement planning. Outliving your retirement savings—known as longevity risk—is a legitimate concern. Developing a plan to mitigate this risk is hence crucial.

Annuities can be one way to counter longevity risk. These insurance contracts payout a set amount of income for the rest of your life or for a certain period. It comes in various types - immediate, deferred, fixed, and variable annuity. Understand how each one works and select the one that suits your circumstances.

11.5. Leveraging Real Estate

Equity in your primary residence or from rental properties can be leveraged as another retirement income source. Consider downsizing to a smaller home, renting a portion of your property, or selling rental properties to generate extra income. Analyze the costs and benefits carefully since selling, maintaining, or renting properties carry their own tax, maintenance, and legal implications.

11.6. Considering Part-Time Work

Many retirees consider part-time work or freelancing as additional income sources while also keeping them mentally active and socially engaged. This can help stretch out retirement savings and provide more security.

11.7. Building an Emergency Fund

It's advisable to have an emergency fund, enough to cover at least six months of living expenses. It can serve as a buffer for unforeseen costs and help you avoid plunging into your retirement funds in such scenarios.

11.8. Adjusting Lifestyle and Expenses

Retiring doesn't mean you abruptly stop adjusting your budget. Continue evaluating your expenses regularly and adjust as per your retirement lifestyle. Make plans for travel and recreational activities, but also factor in healthcare costs and inflation.

11.9. Utilizing Strategic Withdrawal Plans

Formulate strategic withdrawal plans to make your money last. A common rule of thumb is the 4% rule, which has you withdraw 4% of your retirement funds during the first year, and adjust every subsequent year accounting for inflation.

Managing your retirement income is a continuous process that requires regular attention, adjustment and evaluation. Involving a financial advisor can make the process less daunting and more efficient. The aim is to not just live, but thrive in your golden years.

Remember, this is your time. So plan well, stay informed, and enjoy the journey towards achieving the retirement dream.